CENGAGE Learning

Drama for Students, Volume 8

Staff

Editorial: David M. Galens, *Editor.* Andrea Henry, Mark Milne, and Kathleen Wilson, *Contributing Editors.* James Draper, *Managing Editor.* David Galens, *"For Students" Line Coordinator.*

Research: Victoria B. Cariappa, *Research Manager.* Andrew Guy Malonis, Barbara McNeil, Gary J. Oudersluys, Maureen Richards, and Cheryl L. Warnock, *Research Specialists.* Patricia Tsune Ballard, Wendy K. Festerling, Tamara C. Nott, Tracie A. Richardson, Corrine A. Stocker, and Robert Whaley, *Research Associates.* Phyllis J. Blackman, Tim Lehnerer, and Patricia L. Love, *Research Assistants.*

Permissions: Maria Franklin, *Permissions Manager.* Kimberly F. Smilay, *Permissions Specialist.* Kelly A. Quin, *Permissions Associate.* Sandra K. Gore, *Permissions Assistant.*

Graphic Services: Randy Bassett, *Image Database Supervisor.* Robert Duncan and Michael Logusz, *Imaging Specialists.* Pamela A. Reed, *Imaging Coordinator.* Gary Leach, *Macintosh Artist.*

Product Design: Cynthia Baldwin, *Product Design Manager.* Cover Design: Michelle DiMercurio, *Art Director.* Page Design: Pamela A. E. Galbreath, *Senior Art Director.*

Copyright Notice

following: unique and original selection, coordination, expression, arrangement, and classification of information. All rights to this publication will be vigorously defended.

Saved

Edward Bond

1965

Introduction

Saved was first presented on November 3, 1965, at the Royal Court Theatre, London, as a private club production of the English Stage Society. The "club" designation was necessary because the Lord Chamberlain, the head of the Queen's household and the official censor of British theatre, had demanded such substantial alterations to the text before granting a license for performance that the Royal Court had decided to dodge the law in order to present the play as written and without a license. It had long been held that the Lord Chamberlain did not have authority over "private" club productions.

The production caused an uproar. On opening night there were shouts of outrage from the audience and physical violence in the foyers during the intermission and after the show. *Saved* explores the dehumanizing industrial environment and the moral emptiness of the working-class world of South London and the beastliness and brutality that are the result. The scene that most shocked the audience and to which the Lord Chamberlain had objected with no room for compromise involved the murder of a bastard baby in its pram by a group of young working-class louts, including its father. Most of the critics, with such prominent exceptions as Martin Esslin, Penelope Gilliatt, and Alan Brien, "slaughtered" the play. Aroused patrons formed "representative" organizations to fight such "obscene," "sadistic," "filthy," and "unfunny" drama. Leaders of the Royal Court were arrested on a technicality of the law (police officers, who were members of the English Stage Company, were not required to show their cards when entering the theatre) and there was a court case.

Although the Lord Chamberlain made it clear that he did not intend to challenge the right of private clubs to present plays that had not been approved by his office, the Magistrate's decision stated clearly that the Lord Chamberlain did in fact have jurisdiction over such productions. That closed the door on what had always been seen as an outlet for *avant garde* theatre to be performed free of censorship. The *Saved* case was thus directly instrumental in ending pre-production censorship in England, which officially occurred on September 28, 1968. *{Early Morning,* Bond's next play, was the last play to be banned *in toto* by the Lord Chamberlain.) One of the first results of the demise of the censor was a short repertory season of Bond plays at the Royal Court—*Saved, Narrow Road to the Deep North,* and *Early Morning.* The abolition of the censor by the Theatres Act of 1968 allowed the whole of theatre to deal seriously with contemporary reality in an adult manner.

Author Biography

Edward Bond was born in 1934 into a working-class family in Holloway, North London. In 1940 he was evacuated to Cornwall and subsequently to his grandparents in Ely, Cambridgeshire. In 1944 he returned to London and attended Crouch End Secondary Modern School, where he was not thought good enough to take the eleven-plus exam, which was necessary in order for him to continue school. He therefore left school at age fifteen, ending his formal education. However, while still in school, he went to see Donald Wolfit's production of *Macbeth,* which had a profound impact on him. He later said in an interview, quoted in *Bond: A Study of His Works:* "for the very first time... I met somebody who was actually talking about my problems, the life I'd been living, the political society around me... I knew all those people, they were in the street or in the newspapers this (Macbeth) in fact was my world." He also attended the music hall regularly (his sister was a magician's assistant), which taught him theatrical builds and timing.

In 1953 Bond began his two years National Service and while in the army began his first serious writing. In 1958 he submitted two plays to the newly-formed English Stage Company at the Royal Court Theatre, London, and both were rejected. However, he was invited to join the Writers Group at the Royal Court, under the leadership of the young director William Gaskill, and in 1960 he became a play-reader at the Court. On December 9, 1962, *The Pope's Wedding* was given a single performance in a Sunday night "production without decor" at the Court, the first performance of a play by Bond. By that time, Bond had written five radio plays, two television plays, and seven plays for the theatre, all of which had been rejected. In 1964, *Saved* was accepted for production by the Royal Court, which duly submitted it to the Lord Chamberlain's Office, then charged with the licensing of plays. When the Lord Chamberlain demanded many substantial cuts and changes to the script, the Royal Court declared itself a private club theatre for the production of *Saved,* which opened on November 3, 1965. Bond was finally able to become a full-time writer.

Bond has been a prolific writer. He has written thirty-one plays that have been produced, four screenplays, two books of poems and songs, and adaptations of classics such as Chekhov's *The Three Sisters andThe Cherry Orchard.* His plays have been translated into twenty-five languages and have had productions throughout the world. In 1977 Edward Bond accepted an Honorary Doctorate from Yale University.

Plot Summary

Scene One

The play opens in the living-room. Pam has brought Len home for sex. She insists on using the living-room because her bed isn't made. They have just met and when Len asks Pam her name, she says, "Yer ain' arf nosey." They have trouble getting comfortable. Harry, her father, comes in and goes out again. Len is somewhat disconcerted, but Pam doesn't seem to mind the interruption at all. Pam and Len continue their sex play, Harry again puts his head in, and Pam and Len offer him candy (laced with sexual innuendo). Finally, they hear Harry leave the house for work and as Pam undoes Len's belt, Len says, "This is the life."

Scene Two

Scene Two takes place in a park near the flat. Len and Pam are in a boat on an otherwise bare stage. The audience learns that Len is now a boarder in the flat. They also speak of their relationship, the fact that Harry and Mary haven't spoken in so many years Pam can't remember when the silence started or why, that they had a boy during World War II and that he was killed by a bomb in this park. Fred, the boat handler, calls them in and makes crude sexual jokes. Len jokes back, and it is obvious that Pam is attracted to Fred.

Scene Three

Pete, Barry, Mike, and Colin meet in the park. Pete is dressed in a suit because he is going to the funeral of a boy he killed with his van—intentionally, he says. He openly seeks the admiration of the others and they do admire him for the killing and the fact that he got away with it. They tease Barry and there is lots of low and crude sexual humor. Len comes in and Colin recognizes him from school years before. Mary enters with groceries, Len goes to help her, and there are more crude sexual jokes among the gang.

Scene Four

Scene Four takes place in the living-room. Mary puts food on the table, Len eats, and Harry dozes in the armchair. Pam enters in her slip, turns on the TV and puts on makeup. The TV doesn't work properly and no one knows how to adjust it. The baby starts to cry off-stage and continues to cry throughout the scene. No one does anything to comfort the baby. The only other actions consists of bickering about where Pam should dress and small domestic concerns. Fred arrives and Pam nags him about being late and they leave, Len clears the table and Harry tells Len it is better for him to sleep with his door closed so he won't hear Pam and Fred in her room. The baby continues to scream uncomforted.

Scene Five

Pam is sick in bed and Len tries to comfort her. She is pining for Fred, who has dumped her. Len fetches the baby and Pam wants nothing to do with it; she hasn't looked at it for weeks. (It is worth noting that throughout the play the baby is referred to only as "it" by all the other characters.) Len has bribed Fred with tickets for a football game so he will visit Pam.

Scene Six

The park. Fred is fishing and chatting with Len about his equipment and how to bait a hook—all done with cheap sexual innuendo. Len has been fired from his job for staying away from work to care for Pam. Pam comes in with the baby in its pram. She tries to make Fred promise to call on her and he evades her. The baby is drugged with aspirin to keep it quiet and it has had pneumonia once. Pam stamps out in a fit of temper, leaving the baby there, and Len goes after Pam. One by one the rest of the gang wander on talking about sex and making cheap jokes. Barry spots the baby and after violently shoving the pram at Pete, they begin to tease the baby by pinching it. The others, including Fred, join in pinching it, spitting on it, rubbing its face in its own excrement, and finally stoning it to death. After they leave, Pam returns and wheels the pram off without looking into it.

Scene Seven

Fred is in a jail cell and Pam visits him. Fred is outraged because he was attacked by a group of housewives when being brought to jail. Pam feels no animus towards Fred and Fred feels no responsibility for the murder of the baby. He blames Pam for having the baby in the first place and for bringing it to the park. He blames gangs of vandals and even blames the police for not doing their job and stopping the murder. Len brings cigarettes to Fred and, after Pam leaves, tells Fred that he had watched the whole thing.

Scene Eight

Harry is ironing clothes in the living-room and chatting with Len. Len has a job again and Pam is still obsessed with Fred. Pam enters drying her hair and immediately accuses Harry and Len of stealing her *Radio Times* magazine. She and Len engage in a silly but verbally violent spat.

Scene Nine

Len is in the living-room cleaning his shoes when Mary enters in her slip and gets ready to go to the movies with a friend. Mary tells Len to feel free to take women to his room. She tears her stocking near the top and asks Len to sew it while she still has it on. While he is sewing them, Harry enters. He watches Len and Mary and then leaves. Len asks Mary to stay in for the evening, but she says she must go.

Scene Ten

Len and Pam are sitting at a table in a cafe waiting for Fred to arrive with his mates for a breakfast to celebrate his release from prison. Pam tries to get Len to leave but he won't go. Fred enters accompanied by the gang and his new girl, Liz. The jokes are still cheaply sexual and stale. Pam attempts to force herself on Fred and is dismissed and humiliated. Liz continually asks Fred what it is like "inside." Len asks Fred what it felt like when he was killing the baby. Finally, the gang and Liz go off and Len tries once more to reconcile with Pam and once more is rebuffed.

Scene Eleven

In the living-room. The table is set for tea. Mary claims the teapot is hers and pours Harry's cup of tea on the floor. They have a verbal fight in which Mary claims most of the things in the house are hers and Harry accuses Mary of being "filthy" with Len. Mary hits him in the head with the teapot. When Harry tells Pam the fight was because Len had Mary's dress up, Len shakes him and Pam cries and blames all her troubles—even the death of the baby—on Len. Len says he will move out.

Scene Twelve

Len is on the floor of his bedroom listening to

Pam in the room below. Harry enters dressed in white long underwear and white socks with his head in a skull cap of bandages. Harry has come to say goodnight. Len says he never touched Mary and when he points out that Harry and Mary had a row over it, Harry says, "She had a row." Harry talks of his time in World War II. He remembers it mostly as peace and quiet with a couple of blow-ups. He asks Len not to move out. Harry plans to move out, but when it suits him, not Mary. In the meantime, he will retreat to his room more.

Scene Thirteen

The living-room. Len is fixing a chair, Mary is clearing the table, Pam sits on the couch reading her *Radio Times,* and Harry is filling out his football betting slip. The only dialogue in the scene is when Len asks Pam to fetch his hammer. She does not. Len continues trying to fix the chair and the others continue their empty activities.

Characters

Barry

Barry, age twenty and described as a little below medium height and fat, is one of the working-class louts who hang around together in South London. There is little to distinguish Barry from his friends, but it is he who leads the assault on the baby in scene six and who throws the last stone at the baby at point blank range.

Colin

Colin, age eighteen, has "shiny ears, curved featureless face" and "shouts to make himself heard." He is one of the group of male working-class layabouts centered around Fred.

Fred

Fred, age twenty-one, blond, good looking, and powerfully built, is the man Pam becomes obsessed with and who she claims is the father of her baby. Although he is only one of the gang that murders the baby in the park, Fred is the one who is charged and who goes to jail. Still, Fred feels he is not guilty of a crime because "It were only a kid." Fred, like the others, is never able to see the baby as a human being. Women are very attracted to Fred and he has a new woman, Liz, waiting for him when he is released from jail.

Harry

Harry, Pam's father and Mary's husband, is silent for most of the play. Harry fought in World War II and now holds a non-descript night job. He and Mary have not spoken for years, and when they do speak it is to engage in a violent row in which Mary breaks a teapot on Harry's head. Near the end of the play, Harry does open up to a certain degree with Len and begs him not to move out of the house.

Len

Len is the central character of the play. He is twenty-one, "tall, slim, firm, bony," and he works at various jobs as a laborer. Pam brings him home to have sex in scene one and he stays as a boarder. Len is good natured and determined to be helpful, even to the extent of trying to reconcile Fred with Pam, even though he is still in love with Pam himself. Len is not a noble character he is a product of his society, which does not allow nobility and he does not rise above the arid culture of his South London working class background. Len does, however, hold on to his human values of compassion and tolerance, and he does refuse to surrender to the bleak spiritual and moral degradation of the other characters.

Liz

Liz, who appears in only one scene, is an empty slut who is awaiting Fred when he is released from prison.

Mary

Mary, Pam's mother, is fifty-three, short with bulky breasts, big thighs, and "curled gray hair that looks as if it is in a hair-net. Homely." She and her husband Harry have not spoken for many years, though neither seems to remember the cause. Mary is not a warm mother-figure, however. She claims to feel pity for the crying baby but does nothing to comfort it; she bashes Harry on the head with a teapot; she partakes in a highly sexual scene with Len. She is as empty of human values as her daughter, Pam.

Mike

Mike is another of the gang of inarticulate louts and is practically indistinguishable from his mates.

Pam

Pam, age twenty-three, is the central female character in the play. She seduces Len in the livingroom of the flat she shares with her parents, Harry and Mary. She is unperturbed when her father comes into the room. Although Len falls in love with her and stays on as a boarder, Pam quickly tires of Len and falls for Fred. She takes Fred to her room for sex, knowing that the rest of the family, including Len, are listening. She has a baby, claiming Fred as the father, but never recognizes it as human. She apparently feels no remorse when the baby is murdered and remains obsessed with Fred. She meets him on his release from prison, offers him her room to stay in, and is rejected. Pam is the epitome of those whom Max Le Blond in the *Dictionary of Literary Biography* says are "condemned to crawl like lice on the underbelly of the welfare state." She ends the play in silence, studying her *Radio Times* and dumbly facing an empty future which she is too inarticulate to contemplate.

Pete

Pete, at age twenty-five, is the oldest of the gang of louts and represents the epitome of their aspirations. His only real distinction is that he has killed a boy with his truck, an act that he claims to have committed deliberately. He seeks admiration from the rest of the group and he receives that admiration. He initiates much of the brutality in the murder of the baby.

Themes

Alienation and Loneliness

All of the characters in *Saved* suffer alienation from the natural world, from each other, from their work, and from society as a whole; the result is extreme loneliness. The stoning of the baby is only an extreme example of the alienation from all that is natural—the continuation of the species—and humane: no one even recognizes that the baby *is* human. Len is the only character who seems to retain even the *capacity* for compassion, the only one who continues to reach out to others. Nothing illustrates Len's loneliness more than his asking Fred what he has that makes Pam so in love with him. There is slight hope: in his bumbling way Harry does reach out and asks Len not to leave their household. Len is the only human they know and he is needed if the rest are to continue to exist at all.

Anger and Hatred

Anger and hatred are the results of the alienation felt by the characters towards all areas of their lives. These feelings are expressed throughout the play: Pete's killing of the boy; Mary and Harry's long lasting silence and the violence that takes place when that silence is broken; Pam's diatribe over her missing magazine; the stoning of the baby. Perhaps even more frightful than the outbursts is the seething fury that the family represses all the time and which is especially evident in the final, silent, scene.

Guilt and Innocence

The murder of the baby, obviously, represents the Biblical Slaughter of the Innocents. Assigning guilt for that act, however, is no simple matter. Fred accepts the penalty, but not out of any sense of guilt: he blames Pam for leaving the baby in the park and for having it in the first place; he blames "roving gangs;" he blames the police for not doing their job. Fred accepts the punishment because that makes him a hero of the criminal class, which he sees operating all around him in all areas of his life. Pete feels no guilt for killing the boy with his van, and he is admired for getting away with it by the others. Harry feels no guilt for killing the soldier in the war and even considers himself "one of the lucky ones" for having had the experience. There is no guilt assigned for the baby, Harry and Mary's son, who was killed by a bomb in the park during the war. Bond places the guilt for the actions of his characters squarely on the society as a whole for having created the inhuman conditions in which they live.

Limitations and Opportunities

There are no opportunities for the characters in *Saved.* They are limited by their births: they were born into the working class of South London; they have very limited education; they have no contact with the larger culture; and they are inarticulate even about their own lives. Len works at two or three different jobs during the course of the play, but they are interchangeable and not worth talking about; Harry goes off to work, but won't talk about it; Fred is in charge of boat rentals; Pete drives a van. Work is something which holds no interest for those who do it and it provides no benefits except small pay. The lack of meaningful work is part of the reason the characters are alienated from their own lives.

Love and Passion

Although *Saved* deals with sexual partnerings, there is little passion and even less love involved. Len and Pam don't even know each others' names when they first start to have sex. They even joke with one another about how many others they have had. Fred uses Pam but never expresses feelings of love or demonstrates passion. Harry and Mary no longer even speak but there never seems to have been a time when they felt love, and Harry talks of sex as something that is "up to the man." Even Pam's obsession with Fred would be hard to construe as love. Only Len seems to feel love and to express it through a desire to give and to care for others.

Morals and Morality

Morals and morality as an inherent social

guide, or even as an abstract guide, do not seem to apply in the society in which *Saved* takes place. Being able to "get away with it" is the criteria for behavior. Pete is admired for killing a boy and not being charged; killing the baby takes place partly because there is no one in authority to see and, as Pete says, "You don't get a chance like this every day." However, Bond is by extension talking about the larger society which condones killing, as Harry did during the war and as his son was killed by a bomb, and which daily kills the spirit of its children.

Science and Technology

Bond sees science and technology, the basis for the industrial society, as the twin evils that have separated mankind from the natural world. There is no longer the satisfaction of creating or even individually contributing for the laborers and factory workers. They have no control over their jobs or how they carry out their work; they never see the end-product as reflecting their efforts. They are forced into regimens that are both physically and psychologically unnatural. Their rewards are material, and even the material is divorced from their understanding and control; i.e., the TV set that they are helpless to adjust. They have become parts of the industrial and technological machine, crowded into an unnatural environment of row houses and government housing that are created to serve the machine; and, the result is that they have lost their humanity. Fred standing in the park with a fishing rod purchased with time payments and fishing in an artificial lake is a powerful image of man's alienation from nature and himself.

Sex

Sex has become an impersonal activity for the characters in *Saved*. Len and Pam use each other in Scene One without even knowing each others' names, and this has apparently happened many times for both of them. Fred uses Pam and then discards her, feeling no responsibility for his actions. The sexual hunt is calculated and impersonal: the church social club and the all-night laundromats are seen as prime hunting grounds. The closest to a humanly warm sexual encounter in *Saved* takes place between Len and Mary when he darns her stocking and becomes aroused. But even there it seems that Mary has calculated just how far she will go and has consciously used Len for her own ego gratification. The alienation of the sexual act from warm human contact is merely one aspect of the dehumanizing lives these people are forced to live.

Topics for Further Study

- How does the British secondary education system differ from that of the United States? Can you think of any changes that might benefit people such as those portrayed in *Saved?*

- What is the "class system" in Britain? Does a class system exist in the United States? Discuss your opinions/ideas.

- Compare *Saved* with a play by other working class writers such as Arnold Wesker or John Osborne (see What Do I Read Next?). Do the characters seem to have the same attributes? Are the worlds they live in the same?

- Edward Bond believes that if people

are crowded together, subjected to too much noise, and feel constantly threatened, they will become violent. Do you think there is merit in this? Can you think of areas near you where people live like that? Do you feel constantly threatened

- Edward Bond thinks that the end product of working on an assembly line is dehumanization. Do you agree?

Violence

Certainly violence occurs in *Saved*. Most of the public outrage was caused by the extreme violence of the baby killing in Scene Six. As Bond says in the introduction to the Methuen edition of *Early Morning,* "I write about violence as naturally as Jane Austin wrote about manners. Violence shapes and obsesses our society... It would be immoral not to write about violence." The violence witnessed in Scene Six is sickening, as is the violence regarding the manner in which Pete killed the boy with his van. Violence is the natural result of the depersonalizing aspects of the society in which it takes place, the physical and psychological twisting of the human to fit the work pattern of the industrialized world, the lack of control over their own lives, the crowding together in a sterile environment with no sense of cultural roots.

Setting

Saved has thirteen scenes with an intermission suggested after the seventh. Six of the scenes are set in the living-room of the flat in the working-class area of South London that is shared by Harry, his wife Mary, and their daughter Pam—and, after the first scene, Len—and two in an attic bedroom in the same flat; three are in a nearby park; one scene is in a jail cell; and one takes place in a cafe. All of the scenes call for very simple settings. The park is a bare stage (with a boat on it for Scene Two). The interior scenes are also very simply represented: a narrow triangle of flats upstage, giving a very enclosed feeling, with the necessary furniture in front of that for the flat; tables and chairs without the upstage flats for the cafe, and a simple jail-door flat for the jail-cell scene. The settings become more claustrophobic as the lives of the characters become more constricted: all of the park scenes are in the first act and four of the living-room scenes and one of the bedroom scenes are in the second act.

Plot

The plot of Saved takes place over a period of about two years. Bond does not show *development* of characters over that time but rather shows *episodes* in the lives of the characters. There is no explanation of what went on during the sometimes considerable time that has elapsed between episodes other than major events: Pam had her baby, Len lost a job, Len got a job, Fred served his time in prison. This lack of detailed accounts of time not shown leads the audience to assume—indeed, to *feel* —that the lives of the characters have continued with the same drab existence. As it accrues, the audience comes to realize that the background is the subject and the episodic actions are only punctuations.

An interesting plot device is the placing of the murder of the baby in the first act. Although the scene is central to the play, by placing it in the first act Bond is able to focus attention on the situation surrounding the murder, rather than focusing on the build-up to the murder. The murder itself is stunningly shocking because it goes against all that society claims to believe: babies are to be protected. But, given the situation, the murder is inevitable and other similar atrocities in the future are also inevitable because no one seems to be seriously affected by it, not even Pam, the baby's mother.

Character Development

With the exception of Len, there is really no character development at all in *Saved* and that is deliberate and part of the point of the play. These characters do not grow, they do not learn from their experiences. Moreover, no explanations are given of their lives or behaviors so that the audience comes to understand their plight. That also is deliberate. As

Malcolm Hay and Philip Roberts point out in *Bond: A Study of His Plays,* "Emotive demands for sympathy from the stage can only muddle the issue. Once you sympathize with somebody, you make excuses for them. If you make excuses for that sort of behavior, then you condone it and then you condone what creates the situation." Bond wants his audience to react to his view of society by taking action and changing the society itself, not by simply feeling compassion for the characters trapped in their hopeless situations. Therefore, the audience is shown effects which, individually and cumulatively, are shocking and the audience must then involve themselves to arrive at the causes.

Language

The language in *Saved* is so authentic that the Hill and Wang edition has twenty-seven footnotes to explain the meaning of words or phrases. Some of the English critics, who do not come from the working-class, had trouble understanding some of the language, but all admitted that it certainly sounded natural enough. However, Bond's language is not simple transcription; it is carefully chosen and shaped to convey the play's motivation and themes. Its short, staccato structure, while basically used as aggression or to defend against the aggression of others, or even simply to keep others away, is also highly poetic and frequently comic. As Richard Scharine has pointed out in *The Plays of Edward Bond,* the characters in *Saved* mistrust words and for them "language as a tool functions only to hold others at a distance."

Compare & Contrast

- 1965: As part of the "Welfare State," the government owned and operated all public transportation, telephone, gas, electric, and water utilities, coal, petroleum, and steel industries. The government was by far the largest employer in the nation.

  Today: All the industries listed above, including the utilities, have been privatized—sold to stockholders—to promote efficiency through greater competition.

- 1965: The United Kingdom was a leading trading nation but functioned as a separate entity financially and economically.

  Today: In 1973, the United Kingdom became part of the European Economic Community (now called the European Union). This created the "Common Market" for economic integration of the member countries of Europe with a gradual increase in political integration.

- 1965: As part of the youth

movement in popular culture, sexual freedom was being promulgated for both men and women.

Today: There is a great deal more sexual freedom in society in general and things are talked about and shown in the popular media that could not have been done in 1965.

- 1965: AIDS had not yet occurred at all and other sexually transmitted diseases were easily treated.

  Today: AIDS has brought about a broad recognition that casual sex can lead to death.

- 1965: The British Broadcasting Company (BBC) provided the only television programming in the United Kingdom and operated two channels.

  Today: BBC continues to produce television programming and now operates four television channels, with plans for a fifth. In addition, there are sixteen commercial program companies and, through home satellite television, there are dozens of channels available.

- 1965: Plays had to receive a license from the Lord Chamberlain before they could be produced for the public. He could demand changes or could ban the play *in toto,* and there was no appeal from his decision.

Today: There is no censorship of theatre. Plays are subject to the same common law provisions against libel and obscenity as are other areas of the media.

Historical Context

In 1948, as a result of several acts of Parliament, Great Britain (the United Kingdom of England, Scotland, Wales, and Northern Ireland) became what has become popularly known as a "Welfare State." The intent was to provide a more equitable distribution of the national wealth and to provide the basic needs of food, shelter, health care, and education for all of the country's citizens. Basic services, such as transportation, telephone, electrical, gas, and water utilities were nationalized, as were the steel, coal, and petroleum industries. While extreme by United States standards, the Welfare State remained basically a capitalist economy.

The class hierarchy, ranging from agrarian workers and urban working-class through the various levels of the middle-class to the established levels of the aristocracy remained in place, although, theoretically, it became easier to move up the social and, especially, the economic scale.

The level of education was dependent upon success in examinations taken at various stages. Edward Bond attended the Crouch End Modern School after World War II and was thought not good enough to take the eleven-plus examination, which, if passed, would have allowed him to progress to grammar school (the equivalent of high school in the United States). Thus, his formal education ended at age fifteen, the level at which the majority of British students ended their formal education and entered the work force.

National Service, known in the United States as the "draft," was required of every able-bodied male for a period of two years.

Elsewhere, the United States began bombing North Vietnam as a general policy and the first deployment of U.S. combat troops in Vietnam took place in 1965. Malcolm X was assassinated. Voter registration marchers were attacked by Alabama police and Federalized National Guard troops were sent in to protect them. President Johnson announced programs for a "Great Society" to eliminate poverty in America. "Early Bird," the world's first commercial satellite, was put into orbit and began to relay telephone messages and television programs between the United States and Europe.

The Arts Council of Great Britain had been established immediately following World War II, providing government funds to support all the arts throughout Great Britain. Although support was meager at first, it did have an enormous impact on making the arts available to everyone. Among those receiving support was the English Stage Company at the Royal Court Theatre in London, formed in 1956 to support playwrights whose work had no chance of finding an initial commercial production. It quickly became the inspiration and the national home for new play writing in Britain. In 1958 the Royal Court formed the "Writer's Group" to work with new writers and Edward Bond, still unproduced, was invited to become part of the group.

In 1965, theatre censorship was still operating under the authority of the Theatres Act of 1843, under which the Lord Chamberlain, head of the Queen's household, was given absolute authority to determine what could and could not be produced on any stage in Great Britain. Plays had to be submitted to his office to receive a license before they could be performed. Stage censorship was an anomaly—a play banned from the stage could be seen by millions on television or heard over the radio. BBC radio and television frequently produced the works of serious playwrights such as Samuel Beckett and Harold Pinter and others who also wrote for theatre. The Rolling Stones, still playing in pubs the year before, had a huge success with *Satisfaction.* In the United States, the Grateful Dead had its beginning in San Francisco; "op" and "pop" art were fashionable; Congress passed legislation creating the National Endowment of the Arts with an initial grant of $2,500,000.

Critical Overview

The critical reaction to *Saved* was, for the most part, a slaughter. Irving Wardle of *The Times (London)* said that "The most charitable interpretation of the play would be as a counterblast to theatrical fashion, stripping off the glamour to show that cruelty *is* disgusting and that domestic naturalism *is* boring. But the writing itself, with its self-admiring jokes and gloating approach to moments of brutality and erotic humiliation does not support this view... it amounts to a systematic degradation of the human animal." Herbert Kretzmer of the *Daily Express* said, "It is peopled with characters who, almost without exception, are foul-mouthed, dirty-minded, illiterate, and barely to be judged on any recognizable human level at all." J. C. Trewin of *The Illustrated London News* said, "It may not be the feeblest thing I have seen on any stage, but it is certainly the nastiest, and contains perhaps the most horrid scene in the contemporary theatre. (Even as I write that hedging perhaps' I delete it: nobody can hedge about *Saved.)*" B. A. Young, critic for *The Financial Times,* despised the play and said, "if such things are really going on in South London they are properly the concern of the police and the magistrates rather than the audience of theatres, even the Royal Court." Even those reviews that were positive were not geared to bring in the audiences. Penelope Gilliatt of *The Observer* gave a thoughtful and positive review; but it started with 'I spent a lot of the first act shaking with claustrophobia and thinking I was going to be sick. The scene where a baby in a pram is pelted to death by a gang is nauseating. The swagger of the sex jokes is almost worse." Alan Brien of *The Sunday Telegraph* was deeply moved and wrote, "It appears that the British audiences and critics can stomach unlimited helpings of torture, sadism, perversion, murder and bestiality when perpetrated by foreigners upon foreigners in the past.... But when Edward Bond in *Saved* at the Royal Court shows us London youths, here and now, beating and defiling a bastard baby... then a cry goes up to ban and boycott such criminal libels on our national character.... *Saved* makes an unsympathetic, disturbing, wearing, sometimes boring evening in the theatre. But I believe it fulfills one of the basic functions of the drama... that of making us remember the monster behind the mask on every one of us."

Although the box office suffered (fifty percent of the seats were sold and 36.7 percent of the possible box office takings were realized during the entire run), the Royal Court kept the play running. And, many of the most influential of the theatre profession rallied to the cause, including Laurence Olivier. Mary McCarthy, the American author, praised the play for its "remarkable delicacy."

Saved had better receptions abroad. Bond was a favorite in Germany and by March, 1968, *Saved had* had more separate productions in Germany than it had had *performances* in England. It received its

American premiere at the Yale Repertory Theatre in December, 1968, and shortly after had its Canadian premiere at McGill University in Montreal. A retrospective season of Bond plays, including *Saved,* opened at the Royal Court on February 7,1969. The critical reactions were very different for this production. Irving Wardle said, "it is now time for the guilty reviewers to queue up and excuse their past arrogance and obtuseness as best they may. As one of the guiltiest, I am glad to acknowledge that my feeling toward the plays has changed, and that if I had originally responded to them as I do now, I should not have applied words like 'half-baked' and 'untalented' to *Saved* and *Early Morning.*"

Sources

Bond, Edward. *Saved,* Methuen, 1966, pp. 6, 9–10, 11, 19, 69, 75.

Bond, Edward. *Lear,* Eyre Methuen, 1972, p. 5.

Brien, Alan. *The Sunday Telegraph,* November 7, 1965.

Browne, Terry W. *Playwrights' Theatre,* Pitman Publishing, 1975, pp. 56–57, 62-63, 121.

Gilliatt, Penelope. *The Observer,* November 7, 1965.

Hay, Malcolm, and Roberts, Philip. *Bond; A Study of His Plays,* Eyre Methuen, 1980, pp. 15, 48–49, 54, 62.

Kretzmer, Herbert. *The Daily Express,* November 4, 1965.

LeBlond, Max. "Edward Bond: Criticism," *Dictionary of Literary Biography,* Volume 13: *British Dramatists Since World War II,* Gale, 1982, pp. 83–91.

Scharine, Richard. *The Plays of Edward Bond,* Bucknell University Press, 1976, pp. 54, 69.

Thom, Mary V. "Letters," *Plays and Players,* February, 1966, p. 8.

Trewin, J. C. *The Illustrated London News,* November 13, 1965.

Wardle, Irving. *The Times,* November 4, 1965.

Wardle, Irving. "The Edward Bond View of Life," the London *Times,* March 15, 1970.

Young, B. A. *The Financial Times,* November 4, 1965.

Further Reading

Browne, Terry W. *Playwrights' Theatre: The English Stage Company at the Royal Court,* Pitman Publishing, Ltd., 1975.

> Tells the story of the theatre that was primarily responsible for making theatre more socially relevant in post-World War II England. It contains a segment that deals in detail with the first *Saved* production and the ensuing court case.

Cohn, Ruby. *Retreats from Realism in Recent English Drama,* Cambridge University Press, 1991.

> Deals with developments of British Drama since about 1965, including works by Edward Bond. It gives a good overview and covers briefly such critical movements as post-modernism.

Dictionary of Literary Biography, Volumes 13 & 14: *British Dramatists Since World War II,* Gale, 1982.

> This excellent compilation contains entries on every major British dramatist since World War II and also includes articles on the Arts Council of Great Britain and all the major subsidized companies.

Hall, Edward T. *The Hidden Dimension,* Doubleday & Company, Inc., 1966.

> Studies the social and physical pathologies that result from too little physical living space for people.

Hay, Malcolm, and Roberts, Philip. *Bond, A Study of His Plays,* Eyre Methuen, 1980.

> The authors were given unrestricted access to Bond's correspondence, notes, rough drafts, and unpublished plays for their superb study of his work. They have also interviewed directors, designers, and others who worked on productions of his plays.

Hay, Malcolm, editor. *Bond on File,* Methuen, 1985.

> This small volume includes excerpted reviews, performance history, and a selection of Bond's own comments on his work.

Hobson, Harold. *Theatre In Britain, 1920-1983* Phaidon Press Limited, 1984.

> Harold Hobson, for many years the dean of English drama critics, gives an overview of his sixty-three years of attending theatre. This serves as a solid background about what was going on in general, and especially in the commercial theatre, in England during the time Edward Bond and

others were developing and writing.

Scharine, Richard. *The Plays of Edward Bond,* Bucknell University Press; Associated University Press, 1976.

> This is an excellent study of Bond's early works, through *The Sea,* 1973. It includes a section on techniques and themes which can be applied to Bond's later works as well.

Lightning Source UK Ltd.
Milton Keynes UK
UKHW021854120121
376897UK00009B/305